TRUTHFAIRY FIELD GUIDE: NO GURU REQUIRED

A PASSIONATE JOURNEY TO YOUR PRECIOUS TRUTH

DONNA SYED

BE. DO. LIVE. BOOKS
An imprint of North Arrow Publishing

READ THIS FIRST

only human, and can only speak to my own memory, perception, and experience of other people and circumstances. If at any point I deemed it was necessary, I have changed names, details, and determining characteristics of people and places to avoid hurting anyone. I also present myself as a character, persona, or omniscient narrator-in-retrospect, either for the benefit of the subject matter, in context of the stories I narrate, or in those I make reference to, that are relevant to this book's objective which lies outside the scope of any personal narrative. With the above in mind, the author expects readers to allow for any unintentional or unknown contextual differences considering personal accounts and stories. Choosing to read any part of this book beyond this point constitutes your understanding of and agreement with the above.

Published by North Arrow Publishing | Be. Do. Live.

Printed in the United States of America

Library of Congress Control Number: 2017917171

ISBN 978-0-9963523-2-1

10 9 8 7 6 5 4 3 2 1

Developmental Editing: The Michelle K

Proof Review Editing: Dr. Cristy Lopez

First Edition

Syed, Donna, author

Truthfairy field guide : no guru required

Woman/Donna Syed.

Issued in print.

ISBN 978-0-9963523-2-1 (softcover)

1. Self-actualization (Psychology) in women. 2. Women—Life
skills guides. 3. Women—Psychology. I. Title.

PSSST!

Before we get started, I've got something for you.

Grab a cup of Real Life Tea and meet other women who are already reading this book. We're getting together for *actual* coffeehouse chats, *and* we're meeting up online to be seen, known, and heard as we each step stronger and higher.

We're all on this journey together. Come with us.

TRUTHFAIRYEXPERIENCE.COM

We're all showing up to get and give sage wisdom, much of it brewed straight from the conversations we have in our brand-new (and cozy) global community.

~

JOIN IN WITH
POWERFUL WOMEN
REAL CONVERSATIONS
POP-UP ADVENTURES
BACKSTAGE PEEKS
EARLY ACCESS

Let's do this.
www.TRUTHFAIRYEXPERIENCE.com

WHAT I KNOW FOR SURE IS THAT SPEAKING YOUR TRUTH IS THE MOST POWERFUL TOOL WE ALL HAVE.

—*OPRAH WINFREY*—

Receiving the 2018 Cecil B. DeMille Award

∾

Amen, my Spirit Auntie, Amen.

CONTENTS

ACKNOWLEDGEMENTS

First, I want to be clear:

It's tough to thank (and impossible to forget) those who, at one time or another, without mercy or kindness, challenged everything I believed about Truth; so instead, I'll simply acknowledge their contribution to the tangles that I would not surrender to.

Clarity, strength and discernment are the fruits of that labor.

Mascara streams are already starting to roll down my face just thinking about these next precious souls, because love is like that sometimes.

Now, here goes . . .

But for the guidance, depth of knowledge, and investment of wisdom from Ms. Zaina Ali, *Queen Neefa Feefa*, my journey through this life might have taken a very wonky turn at Albuquerque and I would be somewhere completely different. She shepherded my soul Northward with a wisdom and compassion too precious for this world. I'm grateful for the scenery this path has taken me. The view is magical.

In this moment, I find myself in gratitude for the many

thoughts, writings, research and hieroglyphs that those who came before me took the notion to write down.

Without thinkers and explorers like Dr. Abraham Maslow (my first dead guy crush), Dr. John Nash, Dr. Mihaly Csik-szentmihalyi, Dr. Jane Bolte Taylor, Dr. Bessel van der Kolk, Dr. Bruce Perry, et al, I might never have begun to understand the intersection of the human spirit with the functioning of our very human brains.

I also must say something true about a woman who climbs African mountains, ran with the bulls, blazes through Iron Man races, all after conquering cancer—and who, a very long time ago, loved me enough to pull the branches back and show me Truth when I was a little lost in the bushes. But for her, I might never have written anything for anyone to read. Jenne Beecher Fromm, I will always remember you, while we both live and after.

DEDICATION

To my children, know that you inspire and amaze me every single day. I love you, always.

To my husband, who convinced me of True Love, your patience, faith, and steadfast soul takes my breath away.

Sierra and Michelle, my yin and yang Ethels . . . oh, where would I be without you?

And, to my best good friends, from our boundless laughter to our sweetest tears, you are among the treasures of this Universe. I am blessed and privileged to be in this world with every one of you.

We need to have a slumber party with feet pajamas.

Sweet Mamma Esther, forever and ever, Amen.

And, Donna Stewart who was the first real Truthfairy I ever met.

Dearly Beloved, we are gathered here today,
To get through this thing called life.

—Prince Rogers Nelson

CAN WE TALK?

HAVE YOU EVER ASKED YOURSELF:

"What if I really AM . . . angry? hurt? crazy? desperate? a fool? afraid? unplugged? a liar? unqualified? greedy? materialistic? a fraud? worthless? an alcoholic? unwanted? lazy? stupid? unworthy? trash? unplugged? an addict? a victim? depressed? a horrible mother? too old? too late? to blame?

If you have ever felt accused and charged with guilt when you wished you could plead your innocence, instead of "No Contest" and explain what other relevant circumstances led up to all of this–or at the very least, plead some form of temporary insanity—but the charges, words they said, the judgements, the labels that seem to bear no expiration based upon kernels of truth or untruth laced with venom and slung about like straightjackets . . .

And now you're left only with you, questioning you.

Standing there with your toes on the threshold.

Skeleton key in hand.

You have the opportunity to unlock your freedom to choose • purpose • dreams • soul wisdom • passion • illusions • gifts to the world • creative flow • peace • story • potential energy • brilliance motivation • genius • true identity

By Honoring your Truth

Even if it's just a little bit at a time.

That's what happens when you decide to become your own Truthfairy. The good news is, it's safe to tell you the Truth. You're not judgmental. You're kind, you're intelligent, and you're compassionate.

And the best part is, you know your story better than anyone.

Does this seem a little intimidating? Maybe even a little scary--or even dangerous? Everything about what has happened up to the moment you made it here, to reading this very WORD, has been more unbelievable than fiction . . . because it's True.

Do you feel that?

That's your Truth outgrowing your fear.

~

The more we get to know one another, the more you'll notice that one of my favorite things to do is tell stories. I spent some years on the theatre stage telling stories through characters other people created, learning their subtext, analyzing their intentions and motivations, exploring the morals and lessons in every twist and turn of a playwright's script. The most prolific actors of our time have sought to tell the story of a character's truth, to "portray them honestly," (also see, authentically) and with a depth that simulates life itself. I like to tell true stories woven with metaphor, and often unexpected, vivid personifications of ideas and thoughts worth weighing. It's how I relate to the world—and most importantly, it's how we relate to one another.

> *My story might be your medicine,*
> *and your story might be mine.*

Whatever brought you to picking up this book— whether it was a gift, an impulse buy, a friend or therapist's recommendation, or because of some time we spent together in a Truthfairy Experience™, an Awaken Women Dance™ growth seminar, a class, or an experiential retreat, the fact that you're reading it right now says something about what you want, what you suspect is true, and what you believe about yourself. It suggests that you are ready for more, ready for something different, something more expanding . . . and maybe even the idea that you just might be more powerful and free than you've ever realized.

Whether it was this book's title, a recommendation, or a dance experience that brought you here, something inside of you is ready for more.

Every question you have is often a statement of your own knowing, or an expression of a desire to explore yourself, and your relationship to others in this world. It's your precious curiosity about who you are and why you're here that keeps you moving toward a deeper understanding of how this all this *being human* thing works. Then sometimes, the kinds of questions we find ourselves wrestling with seem too abstract or tangley to answer. I'm talking about the questions that scroll through your inner thoughts like a slow, steady stream, silently looping in the background of your thoughts like the CNN headline ticker scrolling along the bottom of the screen, waiting for you to respond. You know the ones, the squeaking hamster wheel filler stories that filter through your mind faster and more persistently than a trending Twitter feed.

Is this all there is? • Is there more for me? • Am I doing what I was meant to do? • How will I know what I'm supposed to be doing? • What's my purpose? • Do I matter? • What am I really worth to anyone? • Will anyone ever see or value me for who I really am? • I have so much, and yet, why am I so unsatisfied? • Who am I, really? • If not this, then what? • Can I really have more than this? •

In your quieter moments, these questions may spark an inner conversation that ends up feeling like a cross-examination. These kinds of self-interrogations can sometimes show up as an aggravating whisper and other times they feel like a mighty roar. And, sometimes, they hang around like lonesome companions who seem to enjoy your suffering company after a long or painful ordeal.

No matter how these questions feel or how they show up in your life, once they creep in, they're pretty persistent. And of course, it seems like these niggling questions rise to the surface even faster just when you feel like you have taken on the proverbial last straw.

You can certainly surrender to them and continue on as you were. You do have that choice. You can also choose to shrug your shoulders, drone out on social media, binge-watch eight seasons of anything on Netflix . . .

or, you can take them on.

It might seem like a lot to take on. Maybe too much even, because we know the struggle often begins with the sit-down-and-shut-up statements of evidence against you that your very own *Inner Critical Sniper* comes at you with like a mean girl on the playground.

That's often enough to keep you from inquiring much further.

Sometimes these questions are sneaky and parade around as soul-numbing disqualifiers, meant to lull you back into a droning sleepwalk of your ultimately unsatisfying status quo. Other times, the same questions are paralyzing reminders of past trials, fortune teller tales of impending disaster, character assassinations meant to arrest and squelch your pursuit of feeling vividly purposeful, alive, and in passionate pursuit of a deeply meaningful mission. When these thoughts poke at you, your self-defense can sound flimsy, frivolous, selfish, ridiculous, or plain impossible as doubt-infused messages smother those soft and meaningful questions like a team of smooth, razor-sharp prosecutors who have file boxes full of what *appear* to be solid historical evidence (even if they are just incomplete snippets or purely circumstantial). All of this can leave you feeling like your life is on trial, complete with lists of character witnesses, recorded testimony, statements made by people whose opinions you hold sacred, deem powerful—or once did.

If only there was someone, anyone who knew how to defend you, defend your Truth—assign you a passionate mission, call off those junkyard dogs, and convince you that you are not only capable of carrying out your mission, but worthy of it, complete with a buffet full of joy and heart-swelling triumph that comes with this journey. You were made to experience Love. You are *here*, for Goodness sake.

You do realize there's more to this life than just circling around, right?

So, what if there was someone who knew your capital "T"

Truth--someone willing to honestly consider the full history of your circumstances, your intentions, desires, challenges, struggles, dreams, hopes, confusion, pain, gifts, weaknesses, brilliance, and needs—all in full context, with a depth of compassion equal to the depth of pain that was, or now is. Someone who is willing to engage your powerfully compassionate Truth, acknowledging your shame as deeply as they recognize the dynamically faceted gifts that only *you* have. That kind of Truth, when acknowledged and spoken, produces a powerful, almost magical energy that can and will dissolve the circumstantially incriminating "case" against you that's been holding you back—dismissing all charges, silencing the doubting voices, and commanding them to hold their peace.

Now is a good time to tell you that this becoming a Truthfairy stuff isn't for fakers. It's certainly not a license to indiscriminately run around giving other people an unfiltered piece of your mind when you get your britches in wad all in the name of being a Truthfairy.

We're talking about you—the Truth of You.

It's only fair to tell you that this process is going to take some courage and at times, it can feel a little sideways, or even exhausting. Other times, it will feel as precious as a long-awaited exoneration, a puppy unleashed, or a wild mustang galloping full speed through the surf at dawn. If it sounds intense or even a little intimidating, that's because, you're at the beginning. This is new and a little unfamiliar, and that's okay.

Your first mission, and only if you choose to accept it, is to make a capital "D" decision—but before we get to your Decision, I owe you this:

WARNINGS AND ADMISSIONS

Beginning the Truthfairy Journey is a serious decision that should be weighed carefully.

You cannot un-know your Truth when you have encountered any part of it–you can only pretend not to know.

You are the only one who knows your story and your Truth, what you know, what you feel about it, and what it really means to you.

Your Truth belongs to you.

It is yours to honor, tell, hide or disregard, but whatever you decide, your Truth will wait for you as it always has.

If you're still tracking with me this far, I'm assuming you have Decided and are game to move forward. Which brings me to tell you, I'm glad we're in this world together—because here's a Truth: Every single word of every sentence, of every chapter . . . every breath of every class, of every song, of every dance, of every interview, of every article, each spoken word between us—every last bit of performing, writing, and speaking I do on the subject of dancing the life of your Truth is, first and foremost, a sermon to *myself*.

Every. Single. Time.

All that I have learned, I share. All that I have discovered,

I share. Every woman dancing her dance is a reminder to me of why I survived, why I love, and why I live, and of all the precious life we are here to share with one another in the name of all that is.

I believe we're all here on purpose. Right here, right now, I'm calling all women people who are recovering in their spirit and healing their hearts, who are looking for some peace-filling compassion for themselves and others, and who are in the pursuit of absolute zest in this lifetime.

As the wise Taryn Strong of She Recovers says so rightly, *"We're all recovering from something."*

And because we were all made to be, do, and live our best lives, let's get on with doing just that.

Because we can.

GRADITUDINALS

"Graditudinals" are something I really recommend. Doing your Graditudinals helps you practice receiving others' love (and feeling right about it), and helps you remember those beautiful ones who care and how they have invested in your good, good heart.

These are the same ones who are proud of your accomplishments, cheer the loudest for you (no matter if they're in the flesh or not), the ones who have loved you through all the times you were difficult to be around, or just plain sad. Whether you see them all the time, have never met them in "real life" or they are people you once knew, family who once knew you, or old friends who would toast in your honor at a reunion—these are the people of your Graditudinals.

So, here's mine for today and in some form, every day. The list is small by my own standards, and impossible to measure by volume, but here goes:

Because I'm a woman of deep faith, I must recognize God. My God, what a Universe. This place is amazing, beautiful, treacherous, mysterious, gorgeous, heartbreaking, joyous, and just . . . unfathomable. The people here are truly astounding and the compassionate heroes are legion.

With every intention, let me know them and be among them.

I'm grateful for every companion, every teacher, professor, and author before me whose messages resonated with my Truth like a tuning fork—those who encouraged me to write this, to just write it all down, to not let my lifetime pass by without telling you how worthwhile it continues to be using my life and gifts to bring my passionate dreams into form in ways that can be felt, seen, and experienced by others—in the ways that I hope will help even one other human see themselves as the beautiful soul they truly are. As I write these exact words to you, I'm still dreaming some enormous, heart-swirling dreams full of love and possibility. Dreams I sometimes have to dare myself to hold on to or even speak out-loud. Things that may seem impossible to many, but I see them like Walt envisioned Disneyland—a real place that began Once Upon a Dream.

Now then, here we go.

BECOMING A TRUTHFAIRY

MISSION ONE: Tell yourself one Truth. Just one, little, compassionate Truth you have never said out loud before.

Just tell it to yourself.

Rinse and repeat for the next seven days.

Yes, in a row.

P.S. I'd love to hear about how that went. What did you feel? Did you resist? Did you dive in?

Email me: Truthfairy@TheNorthArrow.com
(Yes, *really.*)

Everything is figureoutable.

-Marie Forleo

PLEASE USE A CLEAN PLATE

Ten seconds on the clock. Here's your question.

Would people say you are:
- a) Too much
- b) Not enough
- c) Just right

What was your reflex answer?
Which one stung the most to think about?
Which one felt the best?
Which ones seem impossible?

Your answers tell a little bit of your story.

Like Goldilocks, you get to choose the one that rests well in your soul because who are those "people" really? I know for sure I'm not for everyone and not everyone is for me either—but that's really okay.

You don't have to make yourself available to everyone just like not everyone is available to you.

And that's also, okay.

What you *can* be is true to who you were designed to be. If you think you don't know who or what that is, you're in abundant company. It's the great big figure-outable most people give up on, sometimes right before they recognize themselves.

Have you taken a moment today to really take your own inventory? What are your favorite bells and whistles? What's your "feature set?"

Here's an example of what I mean.

It's been said that one of my personal features is that I'm funny. I make people laugh every day. I find the funny in all kinds of things. I can't help but take notice of the ironies that show up in ordinary circumstances, and I love to tell true stories.

Also, I love laughing. I do it as often as my sometimes very serious world will allow. In fact, if I go too many days in a row without laughing about something hard enough that doesn't have my forty-seven-year-old-mother-of-four bladder threatening to ruin my fresh yoga pants, I start to get a little cranky. Turns out, laughing is good for mental health, good for the body, and good for the journey, because there are times when you just gotta laugh it all out. There are also times, I've had to cry it all out just as hard, and I still do. I'm a girl who feels all the feels. And, that's . . . okay.

Here's another for-instance, I'm a whole lot gabby with my husband and I sometimes tell him stories while I'm experiencing real-time catharsis—and for his scientist/engineer brain, who just wants to solve all the things, I bet that's a lot to absorb sometimes. His day job is literally "Solution Architect" for networks and, out of sheer habit, he can't help but to try to create a solution for me to get through the occasional briar patches I tangle myself up in sometimes. And, see, I'm not asking for him to design a solution, I just want to be heard, and also hear myself figure things out with someone I trust (and who will let me know if it looks like I'm out in left field, facing the wall, when I should be on third base, running toward home). Certainly, this is a challenge for us both, but we figure it out. And that would be too much for some people.

And, that's alright.

And, how about this? There were so many years I felt I would never be enough until I finished my degree. I probably assumed that more people *thought* I wasn't enough than actually did. When I was younger, the jobs I could land were limited without having a degree, and of course, that added to my *Inner Critical Sniper*'s ammunition pile. I was often paid less than a living wage because I hadn't crossed the next graduation stage. I came to believe, very clearly, that because of that incomplete milestone, I wasn't worth more than any basic un-finished degree pay scale would offer me—because, I thought, no one would ever believe I was enough without it.

It all started to change when I finally asked myself:

Enough for *what*?

I was more than enough to survive things children and grown-ups don't always survive. I was enough to heal from brutal child abuse, parental abduction, and domestic violence. I was still enough to find my father after being his missing little girl for thirteen years, and I was enough to endure his sudden death just four weeks later. I was enough to rise from teen homelessness. I was enough to still take on the most challenging courses my school offered. I was more than enough to still graduate on time, and with my class. I did not fail.

I was more than enough to endure one of the nastiest divorces I've ever heard of (still). I was enough to end a custody war that threw two little girls into an emotional blender they are still recovering from as adults. I was more than enough to preserve my sanity, if only for their sake— even when I wondered if I could.

I was more than enough to build a beautiful women's dance studio beyond what once began in my re-imagined, one-car garage. I was enough to figure out how to rise above my higher education, and my raising, to research neuro-science and human behavior theories that would drive the *Dry Eye Guy* to desperation—just so I could understand.

And, as it turns out, I was even enough to write this book.

True story.

After all these things, and more, I was enough to still love and be loved, even when it was sometimes hard for me to believe in. So far, I've been more than enough, really.

More specifically, I've been PLENTY.

～

I walked into my first buffet restaurant when I was nine years old. Until I was in my late twenties, my body was always solid and reliably svelte, I never really gained much weight that I didn't lose easily. I could eat like a full-grown country boy, and would, if given the means. Can you imagine a girl like me turned loose at a buffet?

ALL-YOU-CAN-EAT
PLEASE USE A CLEAN PLATE

I'll never forget that place. Duff's. It must have been as big as a football field and it seemed to seat hundreds, easily feeding them all from two (*TWO!*) carousels of all the good ol' country food you could dream about eating—rotating by, slowly, under glowing heat lamps. Steamy pan, after steamy pan of fried chicken, butter-whipped mashed potatoes, three kinds of gravy, turkey, roast beef, macaroni and cheese, okra, peas, carrots, and corn (both canned and on-the-cob), barbeque baked beans, red Jello® Ambrosia salad, and cheesy broccoli casserole all saddled up with glistening soft dinner rolls as big as a man's fist. The dessert bar was enough to make a kid forget about the four plates of food they just finished. A soup bowl full of canned chocolate pudding?

Why, yes. Yes, I did.

My step-father would always say he got his money's worth paying my way into that glutton-fest. The truth is, there was always enough to eat at home. Always. Sometimes, if my step-father wasn't having a super-hungry day, there was even plenty at dinner time. We were all given enough to eat on the first round, but my step-father had first dibs at seconds. If he passed them up, I was putting it in my belly as soon as he began walking away from his dirty dishes.

Now, we all know that most people who eat too much food regret it sooner or later. (*Hello, Mirror.*) But what's really interesting when it comes to food is that feeling of *plenty*. Plenty to have, plenty to share, and more than enough to go around, or maybe to just have again the next day—leftovers are a sign of abundance in my world.

Plenty means more than just *enough*.

Plenty describes everything you need to be filled, to feel content, to grow with, to be nourished by, to be comfortable, and to be able to share with others. Unless you have plenty to start with (rather than just enough), someone (or everyone) will have less than enough if they share what they have.

I'm going to suggest that we are PLENTY.

We were designed with plenty of priceless gifts, plenty of interests, plenty of personality, plenty of ingenuity, plenty of unique facets, plenty of what you need to create meaning for yourself and others in this world.

I have to say . . . because you and I are both here together on this page right now, no matter what—you *have* been, and you *are* plenty, too. Just sitting there, you're more than enough for anything you need or want to respond to. You're more than enough to find a way to be what you were designed to be, to do what you were specifically designed to do, and live your life with more meaning and momentum than you even thought was possible. More than enough. Your spirit, your will, your personality, your passion, and your desire for meaning were all "Factory Installed" specifically for life here on Earth, fully loaded with all the best bells and whistles for you to be, do, and live all the way.

I mean, really. Have you met you? It's true.

So here we are, moving forward continuing to strive and thrive. Getting better at things each day. And here I am, writing this whole Truthfairy love letter about it, and on the edge of my seat, designing even more beautiful and expanding experiences to share with women all over the world, building community, encouraging our growth as women, and watching in awe as we all move together toward living what we love and becoming more acquainted with ourselves and each other all the time.

We might as well, don't you think?

BECOMING A TRUTHFAIRY

MISSION TWO: Using a clean plate, I want you to take some inventory of your personal gifts. Write down (with your pen) three of your best features, talents, or superpowers—you know, your "Factory Installed" gifts.

For example, what are you really good at? What do *you* have an eye for, especially? What good stuff are you able to do that maybe other people have said they wished they could do even half as well? What can you do that you just *love*. What good things do people say about you or seem to notice about you? What skill or trait do you have that you would not trade for any other—dare I say, that you're most proud of? Write down all the answers you gave yourself and receive from others.

Bonus Round: In person, ask three (or twenty) people in your real-life world to tell you what gifts they see in you. If that seems like a weird thing to ask the people that you know, tell them you're just curious or you're working on a classified personal assignment (because intrigue is fun).

Turn your wounds into wisdom.
- Oprah Winfrey

TRUTH & TRUST WALK INTO A BAR

Most everyone knows the premise of a 'walked into a bar' joke. The basic syntax is:

So, _____ and _____ walk into a bar . . . presumably, to have a drink, and then *BAM* something weird, ironic or unexpected happens, and the response is usually:

a) a pained groan;
b) an eye-rolling har-de-har;
c) the sound of a lone, aloof cricket chirping in the corner.

Trust is a riddle that can feel as sticky and risky as a tavern floor. You don't need the overhead lights on all the way or broad daylight shining in to know that the 2-Second Rule for dropped food should never apply in a bar. And, after all you have been through with this trust thing, you might feel like trust actually *is* a joke—a cruel, running joke. Maybe you have started to consider or come to believe that betrayal, harm, disappointment, humiliation, and devastation are your "just rewards" for trusting another person. You might be so blistered by trust right now that you've even thrown *yourself* on top of that whole untrustworthy pile of them—because after all, you don't even know if you can trust yourself anymore.

And yet . . . you *want* to—and in many ways, feel as though you must. Which means, in effect, that you want to trust, and in order to do so, you must set yourself up for all of the above if you want to satisfy this seemingly self-destructive instinct, expectation, and even need.

Trust is a form of currency.

The more you trust, the more you are investing, and the more you are hoping it will provide many returns. The returns we are after include esteem, comfort, safety, belonging, being and feeling trusted in return. It boils down to value —the moment you realize that you are dealing with a person whom you feel is trustworthy, it's a relief, isn't it?

Oh, but you can't really feel relief until you feel safe. Until you feel safe, you can't begin to concern yourself with belonging, and you can't really feel a satisfying sense of belonging until you feel it is safe to really be seen by another person— and you won't really feel safe being seen by another person unless you trust them to consistently deliver on certain things. After all, what if one day, after all the investing, and giving, and revealing, and sharing, and exposure, and believing, it turns out that person wasn't at all trustworthy in some terrible, deal-breaking, egregious way.

When something like that happens, it can add up to your life feeling like a three-semi-tractor-trailer, seventeen-car pile-up disaster during Friday evening rush hour that creates pain and problems even Houston can't solve, reverse, or heal.

It's just too bad when other people violate our trust, isn't it? It hurts.

The Truth is, a lot can and does happen (all too frequently, it seems) to people who trust.

SO, WHY TRUST?

If you knew you would never lose, you might sell everything you own on Craigslist, cash-out your savings, stock, what's left of your 401k and take it to Vegas. People who are in basic touch with reality know that you *will* lose your money in Vegas. In fact, unless you're a professional gambler, omnipotent, or lotto-winner-lucky, your odds are worse than abysmal, and you know it going in. Not only that, if you don't know how a roulette table works, know at least the gist of how a poker game goes down, or even the basics of Blackjack, you've tripled-down on your losing odds—and yet, for some reason, with all the glitz, bells, music, and lights, you might still find yourself willing to bet your cab fare on one last big chance to make all your money back.

Welcome to Vegas, baby.

If you're like me, you really value being trusted, precisely because you know how valuable trust is when you offer it to another person. You're also very likely aware that with the honor of trust comes the responsibility of honoring it in return. There would be no reason for me to write this book if everyone we have met or will engage, for personal or business reasons, agreed with the idea of honoring trust. To some, it is simply a means to an end—and honor ain't got nothing to do with it.

Here's what I mean: Everyone who has made it beyond the third grade knows the basic value of trust and a few methods of gaining some form of it from others.

Notice that I didn't say "earn" trust from others—

I said, *gaining.*

Charles Manson was a master at gaining the trust of young hippie girls. Politicians know that trust = vote = their elected power position. Shady used car salesmen, sketchy construction contractors, and even lawyers of the dirt-bag variety usually have a very well-developed and reliable shtick of scripted, polished go-to lines they deliver nearly on autopilot. They may even use profession-specific jargon that can be angled and bolstered to politely highlight your ignorance. The memorized cue card of canned answers full of noncommittal semantics that, when delivered in full orchestration, usually produce a decent return for *them.* Their investment is minimal while they work you over to gain the minimum amount of trust required to get your "yes" on the dotted line or go along with their plan. The worst and probably most skilled of this sort are sexual predators. These kinds of people have one thing in common, they gain *just* enough trust from you to meet their objective no matter what the consequences are for you.

Unfortunately, we've all been tried by Trust Swindlers at some time or another and most of us are pretty familiar with their ways. If you don't recognize them with your ears and eyes, pay attention to how you feel in your belly and chest, and always check what your inner voice is saying—after all, your Inner Voice is a precision instrument, Factory-Installed.

So, let's talk just a little bit more about Trust Swindlers. The common thread with Trust Swindlers is that they have all estimated the value of gaining your trust. If they are pursuing it, you have something they value and want. To them, the value of your trust equals (and is a function of) how much of what *you* have is what they want and need. It's still valuable to them even if your trust is only temporarily harnessed while they offer you the bare minimum (or worse, counterfeit currency) in exchange for *your* trust—which, by the way, should come at a premium. To them, it's worth at least a little song and dance because, hell, it's more than they had going in and it is a great return on their time investment. Be ready, because these kind are usually willing to ride your train for as long as it's taking them the direction they want to go. And like hitchhikers, while they never really expect to get a non-stop lift to their end destination, they stick their thumb out there hoping for the longest, most charitable, and hospitable ride.

The quality of a trusting relationship is a function of how well it meets the needs of the people involved (Thank you, Phil McGraw).

Tell yourself the Truth because we often know more than we might admit to ourselves.

We also know that not everyone defines the value of trust the way we do—to some people, and we've all encountered them, the value of another's trust is equal to their perceived value of having access to what they think *you* can offer them. It could be anything: financial, personal, or psycho-social resources. Personal or professional leverage, even for a short-term, one-way use (read: abuse). The idea that **respect**, **responsibility**, and **honesty** are (and ought to be) the minimum price of admission to your life is something you already know. We're not talking about the premium seats or backstage passes here; with trust comes responsibility—and, if you're like me, you want to meet that responsibility. Meeting your responsibility in a trust-based relationship means living up to the basic agreements that trust should require.

Can I get some hands in the air for more integrity?

The interesting thing about trust agreements is that most of them are unspoken, implied, and sometimes, not known or even alluded to, which also makes them very easy for those lacking a moral compass to disregard and claim "no fault" upon indictment.

Here's the deal: Whatever those trust agreements are made of, you are 100% responsible for defining, inquiring about and agreeing to stand by, as well as honoring what is required by others to remain in their trust. Otherwise, you must be willing to re-negotiate the terms or cut your losses, step away, and end it altogether . . . but all this involves being willing to tell yourself the Truth about what you know.

Now that you've made it this far, we're going to dive into your own Trust Policy. If you haven't thought about what your basic Trust Policy is, I have some categories for you to consider and while you're at it, choose the one that resonates with you the most.

COMMON TRUST POLICIES

1. I basically trust everyone. Everyone deserves to be trusted.

2. I trust everyone until they give me a reason not to.

3. I don't trust anyone, really—and I don't let them forget it.

4. I don't trust anyone until they have done enough to prove they are trustworthy.

5. I trust people because other people seem to trust them— mostly because I think I'm a terrible judge of character.

6. I trust my instincts with the people, places, things, and ideas (basically, most things that require a capital letter). I note my initial gut-check estimations, and keep my eyes wide open and my antennae on.

Recognize yourself (or anyone you know) in this list?

Now, match them up with the corresponding number on the Trust Policy Interpretations list

TRUST POLICY INTERPRETATIONS

1. *Ummm, value of my trust?* I trust everyone and especially, anyone who wants me to trust them because I like to be liked and everybody feels liked when they are trusted—and I don't want anyone to feel like I don't like them because I am a really nice person and I want everyone to like me—thanks for asking! I've got to run now, though, sorry! I've got to catch a flight—I'm going to Vegas!

2. *I double dog dare you to do something to betray me*—I may not tell you exactly what my deal-breakers are but you'll sure as hell know it when I let you know it because you should've known better! It never fails, I trust, and trust, and trust, and trust and it always comes to this. You're done. No more trust for you. I make the rules and I decide when this relationship is over. :: *Click. Dial Tone* ::

3. *Let me just tell you why I don't trust anyone.* I've got a firey good reason. I have trusted people, and every time, almost *every single one* of them have hurt or betrayed me. I used to trust everybody and give everybody a chance for me to trust them and I always end up screwed over. I can't figure out why this keeps happening to me. Why are people such a-holes? Why in this world should I ever really trust anyone—so, just know that I don't trust you but don't leave, okay?

4. *You have got to prove yourself with me.* I've always had to prove myself—my trustworthiness, my value and my right to be here so, if you want to ride with me, you better saddle up. And I'm going to test you, and push you, and test you some more—you know why? I want you to try, indefinitely, until you prove me right. I'll let you know when you've finished picking up the tab for all the other people who have abused my trust in the past. If you don't want to keep trying to prove me wrong, then you don't really care about me at all—and maybe you're just another one of those jerk-faces who leave.

5. *I've been really fooled before and paid big—many times over.* Some of it, I'm still paying for. I trusted so hard and so blindly that I have only myself to blame for any of it. I really thought I was a great judge of character for a long time—I mean, I can see the good in people no matter what but I don't ever see the red flags, I guess. So, I think it's just fine to rely on others' judgment and instincts because, based on results, they are better than mine own.

6. *I can't tell you how many times I have said to myself, "Why didn't I just trust my gut on that/him/her? I remember having a weird feeling about it, and I was right."* and I was pretty sick of that nagging regretsey finger-wagging me in the middle of my mess. I'm still not always paying as much attention to what I'm feeling as I should because if my own Truthfairy were able to testify, she'd swear she tried to poke me in the niggles—you know, niggles right there behind your bellybutton? —but I ignored it because I've been wrong before, and

sometimes I feel like I'm being all judgey and hyper-sensitive when I feel, see or hear things that niggle me. You want the Truth? The Truth is, sometimes I really just don't want to know. There, I said it. I freaking just pretend not to know because . . . well, . . . I mean, . . . you know what I mean, right?

~

These "Trust Policies" and their respective characterizations are not meant to be all-encompassing or exhaustive. They are meant to nudge your own Truthfairy into reviewing and considering your own policies. Everyone flows in and out of many of the Truth Policy archetypes you just read (and will hopefully ponder over). It's completely human to have experienced any or all of them at some time as you've been skipping down your own Yellow Brick Road.

Let me give you some good news.

No matter what has happened in your life, no matter how much your trust has been broken, challenged, abused, or disregarded, . . . you will, deep down under all the rubble, long to feel able and willing to trust other people. Trust between human beings feels good because we really do want to be seen, known, and loved by other people—and without trust, love suffers. The more deeply or often your trust has been betrayed, the less you tend to trust yourself and your own judgement. Now that we've said all this out loud with each other, here's where it turns into good news:

You really can learn to trust yourself again, because, my

dear, that's where it begins.

Start by trusting yourself enough to stay tuned-in, stay aware, and stay willing to respond to your inner voice—the one that's always looking out for you in all the best ways. Trust you, and take good care of you—because you *do* know what's true when you see it, hear it, witness it, or feel it.

Your Inner Voice is a precision instrument

Factory Installed

Let me finish up this chapter by getting back to that bar joke because I know I still haven't given you the rest of it yet. Okay, so here goes.

Truth and Trust Walk into a Bar . . . and, as it turns out, there is no joke, but there *is* a punch line.

You know why?

Because Truth and Trust would never intentionally walk into a dank, dark, shady joint where people often go to pretend not to know.

BECOMING YOUR OWN TRUTHFAIRY

Your next mission is inspired by one of my teachers whom I credit with introducing me, for the very first time (at 31), to the notion that I have real choices when it comes to making my own decisions about trust. It's been more than fourteen years since I was first asked to consider my own trust response when meeting people for the first time.

It changed my life.

MISSION THREE: Make an agreement with yourself. For each person you meet or speak with in the next 24 hours, choose one of the following honest answers you would give them if they asked, "Do you trust me?"

1. I trust you.
2. I don't trust you.
3. I don't know if I trust you.
4. I would rather not say.

You may choose only one answer per person you encounter, and it is recommended that you do not actually verbalize these responses to anyone at this time. This one, again, is just for you.

Let me know how that was for you.

I always try to balance the light with the heavy
- a few tears of human spirit in with the sequins and the fringes.

-Bette Midler

HURTS DOUGHNUT

I was an adventurous *Little Rascals* kind of kid with a side of stubbornness that rivaled most goats. Most of it was probably rooted from seeds of frustration, but because I was funny, I could make the best of things more often than not. Like most people, kids included, we can pass our frustration on to the people around us because, . . . well, we're givers like that.

I grew up with two younger, half-sisters, *Suzie One* and *Suzie Two*. Suzie One is old enough to remember half of my childhood, and Suzie Two, who wasn't born until I was eleven, didn't witness much of it. I remember their childhoods with fondness. They were funny, quirky, interesting, and cute little girls, who, thankfully, to my knowledge, have never experienced overt abuse or trauma growing up.

I had six years on the oldest one, and try as we did to be friends, we were really just two different girls living with the same parents, having experiences of them that were as different as zebra print lycra leggings and burlap underpants. So, as you can imagine, we were viewing the same landscape from two very different view finders—but some things transcend big differences, and as a ten-year-old, the ever-enduring, "Hertz Doughnut" game was as satisfying to me as it was amusing to play with four-year-old, Suzie One.

SCENE

The compact, camel-tan, backseat of a 1979 Dodge Omni. Front windows rolled down two-inches for our two chain-smoking parents to flick ashes from as we made our five-hour drive across the flatlands of mid-Missouri to my step-father's rural county of origin.

Suzie One and I were in the backseat, adhering to the Car Commandment of staying on our own sides of the bench seat, and as far away from one another as possible. As a mother of four, that rule has become a legacy in my own cars.

Me: *Hey, Suzie. Wanna Hertz Doughnut?*
Suzie: *What?*
Me: *Wanna Hertz Doughnut?*
Suzie: *Yyyyeahhhh!*

I donked her in the shoulder with my cartoony kid fist—careful not to hurt. I wasn't in any position to invite retribution from the adult people.

Me: *Hurts don't it!?*
Suzie: *Whaaa? Ayyyoww.*

The adults continued click-clacking their conversation over the spitting static of the AM radio news station while pulling alternate drags from their generic cigarettes. I decided it wasn't funny enough.

Hey, Suzie.
What?
Y'wanna Hertz Doughnut?
Nnnnnnohhh!
No means yes and yes means no! [DONK] *Hurts don't it!?*
Hayyyyyyy!
Hey, Suzie.
Noooo.
Suzie.
What?

She sputtered, choking back a giggle.

Y'wanna Hertz Doughnut?
(No answer.)
Y'wanna Hertz Doughnut, Suzie? They're realllly good!
YES!
Yes? Yes, you wanna Hertz Doughnut? Well, alright then!
[DONK] *Hurts, don't it?!*

We laughed like a pack of chimps and were invited to pipe down back there immediately. Someone was trying to drive.

Suzie One decided to give me a go.

Hey, Donna, you wanna Hertz Doughnut?
YES. Right now!
[DONK]
Hurts don't it?!
Nope.

She tried and tried to get me to follow the ongoing punchline but I just couldn't resist the fun of being impervious to the joke. It was still funny to both of us if not a little frustrating for her pre-Kindergarten camera angle.

I mean, doughnuts aren't painful and everybody likes a surprise doughnut if it's the right kind. Of course, once you eat doughnuts, no matter what kind they are, they love to hang around with you for so much longer than you really planned on. You can always buy bigger pants, because dang, you know . . . *doughnuts.*

So, what do Hertz Doughnuts have to do with becoming a Truthfairy? *Whelll,* there's a pesky little riddle about Truth that caught on so long ago that no one seems to know even how long ago, or who even started saying it and repeating it in the first place.

Before you agree or disagree with anything, or get worried I'm about to crank up my sunshine machine and waste time blowing it up anyone's skirt, let me just say this first.

What if the Truth has just been getting a bad rap all this time?

You might have grown up hearing this same story about Truth that I did. I'm talking about one of the most popular and well-worn myths about Truth. And I say *myth* because mythology is really just a collection of believable (or unbelievable), hand-me-down stories people have told one another over time to help explain or make some sense of their lives, what's happened to them, their family history, their experiences, the nature of things on Earth, or just anything about life they don't quite understand, but feel it would really be helpful if we could all understand better. The kinds of stories that seem to make things easier to comprehend and deal with, or even accept. Of course, sometimes they're just meant to teach, and not meant to be taken literally. Sometimes, as we human beings are known to do, these stories are rearranged, personalized, modified, exaggerated, or just an ancestral fairy tale, generations later, being told as a true story for added flavor. Sometimes important facts might be edited out, cut short, or missing very important balancing ends to the stories or lessons—all of which brings me to that important little two-word story that has been spread about Truth that I'd think we should talk about.

I want to address one of the biggest myths about Truth I was ever told.

Truth hurts.

Who hasn't heard this? And who hasn't been reminded of this (by yourself or others) after experiencing a devastating trust breach or personal loss? As of today, are there 8,940,000

Google results for, "Truth hurts." At least 8.9 million people have taken to the Internet to publish warnings expressed through songs, memes, and personal declarations to convince or support one another in this not-so-fair belief about Truth. All these voices together make it so much easier to justify the notion that, "Truth hurts" as if it is an idea worth spreading and hanging on to.

Here's where this can get a little sticky and tricky to untangle.

Let's start here:
What if we decided that it's true, "Truth hurts?"

If you firmly believe that the Truth hurts, I'm betting Truth seems intimidating, merciless, daunting, and anything but the keys to your own freedom . . . but what if that's just a myth? When I asked a handful of people their *quick-don't-think* reflex answer to, "Truth hurts—true or false?" the first five people I asked in-person answered without hesitation:

Absolutely.
Yes.
Of course.
Yes.
And, Hell, yes.

For most people, their reflexive answers were quickly followed up with attempts to add conditions. Most of them wanted to offer at least some middle of the road testimony that didn't fully blame the Truth for all the pain they had endured over their lifetimes, which still didn't seem to really satisfy any of them. It was like listening to a little Hurts Doughnut roundabout that left them unable to fully agree with their own knee-jerk responses.

Okay, not always.
Definitely, sometimes.
It can, but not every truth, I guess.
I know it does hurt, but you can't change it.

And, how about this: What if (like I did) you grew up in a Christian-professing household and were regularly offered, one of the most well-worn, good ol' fashioned (and usually abbreviated) Biblical quotes about Truth:

The truth will set you free.

So, now we have, '*Truth hurts,*' AND '*The truth will set you free,*' rolling around together in your belief system, competing for the steering wheel.

If we believe these are both true, which, if your ever-and-deeply-absorbent childhood brain was taking in all this critical information and looking for evidence to prove them both right (as brains tend to do), then these two can be a serious monkey puzzle of tangled wire hangers, because, if we hold them both to be true—we have our brain's logic to contend with.

Somewhere in your brain, this ping-pong match might be going on:

'If the truth hurts, and the truth will set me free, it must be true that I must endure pain to become free. Pain is the gateway to freedom. I'll do almost anything to avoid pain (because I have a brain, and brains are designed to avoid or neutralize pain). If I haven't got time for the pain—not even freedom is worth pursuing if I have to endure pain to get it. And if it's true that truth hurts? 'No thank you, not today, (says the brain) I've got better things to do than being set free.'

First of all, I'm going to suggest that more than one person has been innocently offered fragments of truth from scriptures. Pieces and parts of full sentences presented as the whole, removed from context, and sometimes even used as tools of persuasion (well-intended or otherwise).

Your brain's most powerful objective is to keep you alive and on Earth, and to keep your soul connected to your heavy, human flesh. Its primary job is to keep you animated and functioning, intact, and in human form. Healthy human brains want to stay in the *on* position and will do whatever it takes to keep going, even if it requires a stunning override, like fighting, fleeing, or just freezing up and playing dead. It's in our most basic human wiring and programming, and it's really powerful. More than that, it is designed to absorb and remember any information that seems like it would be helpful in keeping us alive and moving in the opposite direction of anything painful, much like an airplane's flight recorder.

I would run from a bear, a snake, or a human predator. If I couldn't do that, I'd fight them. If I couldn't do that, I'd freeze and numb for impact—without any noticeable inner dialogue or decision making. It would be automatic because I believe, and for good reasons, that a bear can turn me into bear and buzzard poop, a snake can kill me, and a human predator can do more harm than any of those animals. It's worth adding that predatory animals operate on instinct, predatory humans operate on intention. Thankfully, our brains can respond swiftly and reliably to what we know and believe, but what about the things that don't seem so life threatening? If everything we believe is stored and sorted for retrieval in our brains, are our emotions a reflection of how much we agree with what we are experiencing in any given moment?

I've done a lot of thinking on Truth and I've decided that neither the distortion of hand-me-down sayings, nor the cherry-picked Bible verses I was offered growing up really told the true and full story about Truth.

Here's something to consider:

It's not the Truth that hurts. It's the disappointment that things aren't what we believed them to be—or what we wanted them to be, or what we believe they should be. The hurt really comes from the feeling of loss and change that are often so painful to reconcile that we are willing to believe the pain is caused by the Truth instead of the giant canyon between what *is* and what we thought it was, what we want it to be, or believe it should be—to avoid pain. Let me be clear, the pain of loss is real. The pain of reconciling what you wish were true (still true, was ever true, or never was true) with what now *is* . . . well, that's some friction that can feel like bone scraping road rash on your very soul. If you've ever had an injury that involved skin and bones, you know for sure that it hurts something fierce and healing comes in stages that are often excruciating. Those kinds of injuries need the time, care, and compassion (from ourselves and others) to heal well. Having a human body and human experiences isn't guaranteed to be pain free, it can be a lot to absorb and to endure, especially when it feels like its wrangling your very soul.

Healing is also part of the being human package.

Pain isn't easy to process. I don't know about you, but the last thing I can imagine while I'm enduring heartbreak is that any of these life losses will feel less painful with time. Sometimes, they require more of you than you thought you had left.

It took me 25 years to heal from the second, and final, loss of my father. I was abducted by my mother from him as a four-year-old after being left behind with him for nearly eight months. One evening, my mother and her friend, wearing full disguises, forced their way into my grandmother's apartment, and snatched me from my bed. I was whisked away and immediately hidden 250 miles from anything I knew or had ever seen before, far from anything or anyone, besides my mother, that I recognized as home. I was allowed no photos of my dad, no way to contact him, and I was made to understand that talking about him in front of my new stepfather was not allowed. Mentioning his name was dangerous. Seeking him out was absolutely forbidden. I now had a new dad, I was told, and calling him "Dad" was an order.

I loved my father, and in secret, I cried for him and prayed he would find me as I experienced ongoing physical and psychological abuse. The Truth is, no one in the house I grew up in seemed concerned for my well-being, except in ways that could be observed or noticed by people outside the home. I was a terrified child who did her best to put on a brave and confident face. I endured the beatings until I couldn't. Thirteen years later, I braved what was forbidden. When I was a senior in high school, a friend I had dared to confide in about my father had gone home that day, and through directory assistance (circa the 1980's), she found my father's phone number and slid it to me across our study hall table the very next afternoon.

Weeks later, I dared again—to secretly meet my father face-to-face. It felt like I was risking my life.

Just thirty days after that, I lost him again to an unpredictable, sudden death. He was forty, I was seventeen.

Weeks after I buried him, I would be asked, very colorfully, to leave the only home I had left.

The Truth didn't hurt me, the Truth was a witness to what did hurt.

It wasn't the Truth of what happened that actually hurt me, I believe it was the people in my life who inflicted abuse and neglect, or who were otherwise stunningly callous to my human beingness that actually hurt me. The tremendous loss, abandonment and confusion was painful. The Truth had nothing to do with it. The Truth is just the testimony. But if you asked me as a child if the Truth hurt, I would have absolutely said yes. My mother was a firm believer in the *Truth hurts,* and she didn't seem to mind repeating herself about it, or proving it. For me, telling the Truth could and did seem to have the power to cause terrorizing events to unfold all while my mother also promoted the Truth as the Bible's gateway to freedom while convincing me that it alone suspended my very Salvation over the flames of Hell.

No wonder the Truth seemed so tangled.

It may be uncomfortable for you to even read about this particular part of my Truth because when terrible things happen to innocent people, especially children, it's hard to digest. No one really wants to imagine that these things happen to children by the people who are supposed to be protectors. None of us really wants to hear that a long-awaited child and parent reunion doesn't seem to end happily ever after. These kinds of stories can be painful to even hear, and they may even be reminders of some of your own pain. But it is not the Truth that's hurting us here, it's the actions of people who behaved in ways that we cannot, in our very souls, understand or approve of. We don't really want to believe that people are capable of treating one another with dishonesty, abuse, disrespect, or disregard. We have a very hard time accepting that these kinds of people, or those they have mistreated, have anything at all in common with us. We truly do want to believe that people are inherently good and we are always looking for evidence to confirm it—that is, if we haven't given up. The Truth is, while you're here on Earth, you will always find evidence for what you believe to be true, and you will always be met with evidence that seems to contradict the things you believe are true, or wish were true, but aren't.

And that's also okay. The sorting out of all these things is part of being a person. It all comes down to your willingness to look at what is.

What *is* can feel shocking.

What *is* can feel liberating.

What *is* can feel painful.

What *is* can feel overwhelming.

What *is* can feel perfect.

At any time.

If you firmly believe that the Truth hurts, I'm betting Truth seems intimidating, merciless, daunting, and anything but the keys to your own freedom. Guess how I know?

What if we let the Truth off the hook for a minute and call the good, good and the hurty things painful and maybe decide that Truth isn't to blame, it's just a witness to what *is*?

It's worth the thought.

BECOMING YOUR OWN TRUTHFAIRY

MISSION FOUR: Write the truest, fullest, most loving sentence about you that has ever been written.

Be generous.

And ... feel free to go back for seconds.

People generally see what they look for,
and hear what they listen for.

-Harper Lee

HELL YES I'M JUDGING YOU

"People who do the parking space pull-through thing are inconsiderate and oblivious to basic courtesy," I've said.

"You know what—no, I'm just going to call it. They're a-holes. A-holes who need a nice low-speed, head-on collision with my expensive-to-repair, hard-earned car—they deserve an asset draining personal injury suit if they ever hurt someone doing that (God forbid). Maybe then, they'll learn just how inconsiderate and careless that is! There oughta be a law." I continue.

"They're all short-sighted, selfish, and entitled. Clearly, common sense was never installed. Total a-holes." I insist to myself as I wait for this reprehensible motorist to clear themselves of my path after another near-collision.

Clearly, I had parking lot issues, and I assumed everyone who heard that rant after the fact would agree with me (or at least, pretend to because of the passionate fire blazing out of my ears).

You see, I was justified, and I would absolutely tell you so like it was my closing argument.

~

Paul, an old friend of mine, always prefaces his rare commentaries about other people very carefully. He'll say something like, "OK, before I say anything about Sally* I'm going to acknowledge my judgements here . . . I experience Sally as _____, _____, and _____," directly followed by the story of what happened between the two of them.

Let's make a clear distinction.

There's a great big difference between saying, "Sally is _____." and, "I experience Sally as _____." When we say we *experience* other people as something or in some particular way, we're really reminding ourselves to take ownership of any accidental or incidentally unfair judgments we have about that person, because the Truth is, we don't know what we don't know about Sally. What's also true is, it is part of our nature to size people up (part survival, part socializing) and try to figure out who they are and what they want from us. All at once (and always) our brains are assessing and sorting millions of pieces of information per second.

For fun, let's use Paul in a story about Sally. Last week, Sally crossed paths with my buddy Paul several times at the grocery store. Sally had been that annoying person throughout the store that he couldn't seem to get away from. She blocked his way down the bread aisle after leaving her cart in the middle of it. Later, she moved *his* cart out of *her* way next to the dairy cooler as he was comparing cheeses. Of course, ten minutes later, she was two people ahead of him in the checkout lane, audibly arguing for the use of an expired coupon. Then, she took out her checkbook. She wrote that check like an angry bumble bee, stopping twice to ask the cashier for the date and the amount. Paul's attention had been on Sally, like it or not, and his brain worked hard to sort out what and who Sally is, and he used the most obvious information available to make that judgement call about Sally. It's a habit our brains tend to have. What Paul couldn't know as he and every other shopper who crossed paths with Sally that day was that Sally was in another world, unplugged, drained, emotionally threadbare, and grieving.

You see, Sally had buried her husband of thirty years just the day before, after caring for him through his three-month battle with throat cancer. Over the series of encounters Paul had with Sally, Paul experienced her as inconsiderate, self-righteous, and a selfish banshee; though, if he knew all there was to know, he would have easily experienced her as frightened, exhausted, and as broken-hearted as a widow can be. That day, she was so distraught she didn't have one ounce of grace left for our friend Paul who, in the parking lot, simply asked her, by name (she has personalized plates) if she wouldn't mind moving her shopping cart from behind his car as she loaded her car with groceries.

It's not *whether* we're judging one another, it's how.

Being willing to consider that you may not have all the

information you need to make a fair judgment of another person is a good place to start. Saying what you really mean is another.

Do I know for sure that people who pull through parking spaces are a-holes?

The Truth is, I do not.
Is it fair for me to say?
Of course not.

Would it help to get in the habit of saying, "I experience that guy as an a-hole!"? I guess if I really *want* to, I can.

Think of it, though. It sometimes requires a pause for me to slow my gears down a little bit with my thinking brain and call things what they are. Is it true that I'm experiencing this guy as an a-hole? Yes. Yes, indeed. It's also up to me to ask myself if it's for sure true, whether it's kind, if it's fair, and if I'm *really* the kind of person that calls people a-holes.

The Truth is, I don't really know if he's really an a-hole, and if I don't really know, how much good am I doing myself (or that guy) by saying it with such conviction that when my brain hears me, and it responds by surging hormones into my system that raise my blood pressure, increase my heart rate, and narrow my blood vessels to prepare me for a parking lot throw down in suburbia? Can you imagine if Mr. Parking Space Pull Through Guy knew what I was thinking about him how he would experience *me*? I'm sure I don't want to know, and in the end, he might be more right than I am.

Let's just say this, right here and plain.

Of course, we're judging each other. *Of course,* we are. It's how we assess one another—but let's also be clear about it. When our judgements about another person are reactive, raging, pissy, or meant to level the proverbial playing field, it might just be about something more than it appears in the moment. It's certainly cause for pause, a little bit of reflection and maybe even a sit-down with yourself. It happens to all of us, and it has happened to everyone. We're typically not very fair with our judgements (not to be confused with instincts).

When I catch myself judging other people (and it takes practice), I try to remember that it is me experiencing them in a particular way. When I notice myself feeling quickly justified (and that weird satisfaction) in making some sweeping, royal proclamation about another person with limited information, it's time to pause and ask myself what I know for sure. You see, we're only able to understand one another as far as we have inquired about them, and if you can't inquire further, claim it as an experience.

There are a lot of times I have to remind myself to look beyond the moment, beyond my experience of another person in a given moment, and inquire within. I often decide it's worth going a little deeper, because if it's snatching me up by the collar, there's probably something important going on inside of myself.

I also want us to remember that none of us is perfect.

We've all unwittingly been a Paul, or a Sally, or that Parking Lot Guy—or like me (the list goes on). I practice acknowledging my judgements as often as possible. It's something you just practice doing. I promise you, if you do, it will make you feel much better and maybe make it a little easier to live in a place where there are other human beings.

* For the record, our gal Sally is a fictional personality; and, also for the record, I have never witnessed my buddy Paul ever describe any person (Sally or otherwise) as an inconsiderate, selfish, banshee, though his own experience may vary.

BECOMING YOUR OWN TRUTHFAIRY

MISSION FIVE: For the next 24 hours, for each person you encounter:
Whether you speak to them or not.
Whether they are family, friend, or stranger.

To *yourself*, simply acknowledge your judgements about each of them as they have your attention.

Yes, you have been through all of this before.
But you have never been beyond it.

-Paulo Coelho, Warrior of the Light

~

THE WITNESS STAND

If you'd like to, please raise your right hand and repeat after me:

I affirm that the evidence that I shall give, shall be the truth, the whole truth and nothing but the truth, so help me God.

That's a big agreement for anyone to make. We abso-freaking-lutely expect witnesses to honor their oath, especially when it involves a trial. In fact, we revere the idea of someone telling the whole truth. We marvel at the notion of someone committing to tell the truth with more than just a super-duper pinky-swear. Cross-my-hear-hope-to-die-stick-a-needle-in-my-eye honesty is what we crave; and yet, for the witness (who is most often not the person on trial) it can feel like that needle in the eye thing might feel better than telling the whole truth (and nothing but the truth) to a room full of lawyers, who can play word semantics like Texas mercenaries leaving honest, innocent witnesses calf-roped by their own words--clotheslined, body slammed, and tied for points. Witnesses are considered expendable and are often jerked-down for sport.

The act of testifying in court is like embarking on a journey over shifting sands. The spectrum stretches from excruciating to liberating, especially when the stakes are high. It's one of those things that you can either imagine, or you know all too well. When we hear someone recite the oath of sworn testimony, we expect them to deliver the truth with the *fully integrated honesty* these very serious circumstances deserve. And yet, even after we hear them promise, we still listen hard with our best good judgement and discernment, while we watch for body language, tone-of-voice, taking everything in with our very precise and monumentally advanced tic-tac-toe logic, along with our own verbal Jenga® skills—all without the willingness to give the benefit of the doubt to anyone (at least, not right away).

When a series of witnesses testify, you may hear what they're saying while you have your own Scooby Doo hunches about who's being honest and who isn't, because even with the oath, we're all still scanning for the slightest bit of deception.

Which sounds more credible, the person who answers:

> *a) Hm. I'm not really sure; or,*
> *b) I do not recall.*

On the flip side, given the intensity of trial, it's nearly impossible for witnesses to be at ease. Their opponents are highly skilled hired guns who are also wordsmithing wizards whose job (or ego) depends upon winning—at any and all costs.

Giving testimony can feel unbearably treacherous, especially when the stakes are high. You may be telling all the truth you know with as much honesty as you can sweep together from every corner of your soul, and it can be taken out of context, flipped and twisted around in order to hang you up by your ankles.

Who in the hell wants to endure that when you're trying to tell the Truth?

No one I know, and it's not fair.

Almost twenty years ago, I was working as an administrative assistant (my old-school boss insisted I was a secretary) for a big City Hall in a very financially diverse pocket of Midwestern suburbia. I worked for the city's Community Development Department, the division in charge of responding to public complaints about trash, debris, tall weeds, junk cars, broken fences, or exposed trash barrels on private neighborhood properties. My boss, a retired Nixon-era Secret Service Agent, was one of those dutiful, right-hand men whose post was often at the front-right fender of the Presidential motorcade. To him, retirement was a state of mind he couldn't subscribe to. Special Agent Jack P. O'Malley was running this code enforcement division, and he was serious.

If you don't know it, Secret Service Agents are actually more than just bodyguards with police training who protect our presidents; at that time, they were also U.S. Treasury detectives who would investigate large, complex crimes involving counterfeit or money laundering operations. They're the Green Berets of bodyguards with investigative skills comparable to the FBI. It's a pretty specific protocol. Pretty sticky. Pretty intense. Pretty hardcore, and probably pretty exciting; but ultimately, very dangerous. They go to the office knowing they could be nailed by surprise gunfire at any given moment.

His training was elite, and though the sun had set fully on his intense, high profile career, he used his surgically precise communication and case building skills with everything he did as a civil servant, translating that intensity to his communications with private citizens whose only crimes were their unawareness, inability, or unwillingness to maintain their personal property to City Code standards. His style often proved to be just a little too much for almost everyone. As a citizen and "secretary" I found the city's rules to be reasonable and reasonably necessary; Retired Special Agent Jack P. O'Malley enforced them like Federal Law.

Of all the bosses and co-workers I'd ever had, this guy was the most colorful. Few people seemed to like him, and in fact, the temp employee who auditioned for the job just the week before I did, left at lunch on her first day without a word, and didn't return. I didn't have the luxury or the courage to do anything but make the job work out for me. As of my first day, I had exactly two weeks to pay the electric bill before it would be shut off. At the time, I had a six-year-old little girl and an unreliable spouse to support and none of us had health insurance. I could get paid in nine days if I stayed—so, no gruff, intimidating, closed-book, old guy was going to keep me from it. I believed there was always a way to make things work, and if all it required was the ability to meet high standards, and figure out how to work with this guy's grizzled personality? *Pffft!* I had already done much harder things, but no one knew any of that.

Though we were approaching the year 2000, Jack O'Malley still used a hand-held cassette recorder to dictate all of his case notes, memos and correspondence to be typed, filed, delivered, or mailed by a "secretary" complete with spoken punctuation, letter, and line spacing.

"Period. Skip down. Paragraph. Indent. Quote."

He did not miss a comma. His case notes were meticulous. His documentation and evidence procedures were puncture proof and he required everyone who worked for him to keep up and miss nothing.

Collecting and compiling evidence was one of his signature superpowers—and narrating the evidence when he was determined to prosecute? That was his invisible weapon.

No matter how Dragnet-Tommy Lee Jones-John Wayne he was, after a few months, I began to see the actual person underneath his bullet proof façade; but the trouble was, he had a really tough time remembering that things didn't have to be so damn serious all the time and that being an intimidating force to be reckoned with wasn't always necessary. It didn't take him too long to figure out that while I respected him, I wasn't scared of him. He was really just an old cowboy with a bad case of leather ass who had lassoed more than his fair share of bad guys. He'd seen a lot, and not much of it wasn't still classified information. Whether it was his training or just an act of his own frustrations taken out on unsuspecting civilians, he could, and often did, snare them with their own words, at times without much context where context could infer meaning that could perhaps make the story-line a little hard to follow without the benefit of more questions.

Then one day, three months into the job, I'd had enough.

Testing-testing-one-two-three-two-one. Hi, Donna, the case number is 99 dash four-thirty-two. Open the case. The date you typed it, dash, all caps—communication with Ms. Judith Comuckle. On zero-seven, fifteen, ninety-nine, comma, at or about 11:30 am, comma, I arrived at the address listed on the complaint to investigate, period. When I knocked on the front door, a woman, comma, who identified herself as Ms. Judith Comuckle, comma, opened the door, period. I introduced myself as O'Malley, comma, explained the nature of the complaint received by the City, comma, and Ms. Comuckle began to cry, period. I clearly explained the action required for abatement, and further explained to Ms. Comuckle that per City Ordinance, comma, she has ten days to comply, period. All caps, case continues pending re-inspection of—

CLICK.
I stopped the cassette.
SNAP.
I snatched the headphones out of my ears and dropped them on my desk.
SQUEEK-BUMP.

I stood up, sending my wheeled office chair to bounce off of the metal filing cabinet behind me. My high heels CLONK-CLONK-CLONK-CLONK'ed across the office suite.

I knocked my first knuckle twice on the door frame of his office as I passed through it, stepping hard, swinging the file folder in my hand, I stood front and center at his overflowing desk.

"Yes, ma'am?"

"Jack, this is the third time I have listened to you describe a woman crying at her front door after you introduced yourself and explained the complaint to them. I am not listening to this anymore."

I had his full attention. He stared up at me over his half-lens tortoise shell reading glasses, expressionless.

He waited.

I swatted my hair back over my shoulder.

"If you make one more woman cry over trash or weeds, I. Will. *Quit.*"

Silence.

"This report is making them sound crazy and hysterical. Everybody deserves the benefit of context, Jack. If you don't know it, let me tell you, you are very imposing and intimidating, and how you are saying what you're saying matters. Those aren't fair facts to leave out of the narrative, sir. Either tell the whole story, or-or just-just be nicer. Alright?"

Silence.

"Alright, then." I say.

"Thank you, ma'am."

What I knew about Jack was that he was someone's dad, someone's husband, and someone's son, so there were people in the world that loved him, and either he had some conscience underneath that stubborn walnut shell, or he didn't want me to quit.

Leaving procedural protocol behind isn't easy because it can seem like a necessary habit, and for the most part, he didn't abandon it, but as far as I know, he didn't make any more women cry on their front porches until he died. What I learned about telling the full story and giving people the circumstantial benefits they deserve (all things considered) before executing judgement was a lesson in extending compassion, for sure.

The Truth is, we don't know what we don't know, and choosing to suspend our judgement is sometimes the most compassionate thing we can do in the world. Does that mean you can't form an opinion about what you already know to be true? Of course not, but right now, we're just talking about recognizing your thought patterns a little bit. If you think there might be more to a person's story, you're probably right.

Learning to extend that same benefit of compassionate context to myself as much as everyone else was a six-hundred level course for me. It wasn't until a few years ago that I really believed that I, myself, also deserved the same.

I can remember the last time I hung up the phone on someone in eye-squinting, bull-snorting, Yosemite Sam frustration. I pressed the very unsatisfying touch-screen hang-up button, and then totally flipped off the phone with both middle fingers as it rested on the kitchen counter.

It was so gracious and so pretty. What a shame I had no audience.

And, it was just a couple of months ago.

Before that day, I couldn't remember how many years it had been since I'd lost my ability to continue a phone call with an actual human being. Two weeks before it happened, I was rolling along, nearing what I thought was the finish line for this book (yes, the one you're reading). I was sure I knew how I was going to wind up this second-to-last chapter, and then, WHAM!

At the hospital, I was called back into an area where I could see my husband through an observation window, he was lying very still just after the doctors had completed an unexpected angiogram, "Mrs. Syed, your husband needs open heart surgery today. It can't wait. We expected this to be a routine outcome, but his condition is more serious than we expected."

Tunnel vision. Instant tears rolling. Dizzying fear.

The absolute love of my entire life, the father and step-father of my children, my best good friend, the best man still on the planet, my beloved, lay in the Heart Cath Lab waiting for me to give the doctors my consent to treat him. The kids were in the waiting room, because after all, we thought this was going to be a routine thing, a stent at the very most, but we went along with it because a cardiologist had a hunch. For almost a year, we had been convinced by his primary care doctor that it was nothing but his gall bladder acting up with referring pain. We expected this to be a false alarm. We all wanted to be there to stand around and wait for him to launch himself out of the hospital bed, head home to kick back on the couch to watch the Royals beat the Orioles on TV that evening. Just the day before, the cardiologist had said he would be back to his everyday life later this week.

What. Is. Happening?!

"Uh. Uhm. Okay. Yes. Please, tell me again . . . show me, um, what was that? I'm, uh-"

"This is what we refer to as The Widow Maker, it's very serious."

My cheeks tingled, my lips went numb.

I called our neighbor friend, a surgeon who had brought my husband to the hospital two days earlier for what *he* believed were more heart related symptoms than gall bladder.

I handed the phone to the cardiologist, who, doctor-to-doctor, explained the circumstances over the speaker phone. The room started to come back into focus for me, and I carried myself out to the waiting room. I couldn't gather myself up enough for any Wonder Woman posturing. My seventeen-year-old daughter, our thirteen-year-old baby girl, and our ten-year-old son saw me stunned, wet-faced, with no words that would come easy.

I called people. I used short sentences with small words. I didn't collapse. My people came. His people came. Our people came. I fought to stay present in every second of every minute, of every hour, as they each pressed by. The seven-hour surgery, the four-hour post-op anesthesia, the drain tubes, the drips, the wires, the monitors, the ICU. His powerful grip wringing my hand as he began to regain consciousness, struggling against the breathing tube. Hearing me. His eyes opening to see. The darkness, the clock, the beeping. The puffing respirator. The EKG.

Seven entire days later, he made it home, out of those woods and delivered to the foot of the next mountain we had to climb.

When you're at the foot of a mountain, you decide to climb it, or not climb it, knowing you could encounter anything either way. If you decide to climb, you may face anything from severe weather, to falling rocks and mean billy goats, defective gear, a mountain lion, or even a full-on avalanche. You hope to make it to the top without getting too hungry, becoming injured, exhausting yourself, or taking a fatal step. You hope for every step upward it will mean one moment closer to breathtaking sunrises, the purest wonders of nature, and some serious spiritual growth by the time you summit. From what I understand, it's usually a mixed bag. Not everything that can happen does happen, but you'll certainly find every good thing you look for. In the end, it proves you that could, and that you did.

Two weeks after my husband made it home from the hospital, everything that needed to happen, was happening. Though my husband (as he does) pulled through each day of his slow recovery to the highest of anyone's expectations, for me, it was like recovering from an earthquake.

Just as felt I was catching my breath, more life stuff happened. Our old, fat, orange stripedy cat ran out of insulin. And, his vet had none. And, it was the weekend. And, the only place I could get that insulin in the whole city was at this emergency veterinarian's office. The entire vial cost $50 and lasts for a month. The Emergency Vet wanted $180 to give him one dose. The truth is, the woman at the Emergency Vet clinic who was explaining this to me from the other end of the phone wasn't rude. She wasn't impatient. She wasn't anything but honest.

Even so, I was outraged. I couldn't believe it. It felt like emotional extortion. Even with a call from our own veterinarian's office, $180 was the "best" they could do.

I hung up on her as hard as I could on a touch-screen phone.

Chances are, she experienced me as an unreasonable, angry, impatient, entitled, and perhaps even irrational pet owner who just couldn't own her part in her pet's health crisis.

There was more to my story than anyone knew, and yet, there I was, losing my patience and hanging up the phone on someone who was merely the messenger, and who also doesn't make the rules.

Behaving that way is against my personal policy, and yet, it happened. My 45-year-old husband couldn't fully shower on his own, much less work, and adding a dying cat crisis and more medical expenses on top of our lives that included what felt like day-to-day survival, caring for our shell-shocked kids, who have a mom who is trying to smile and remain positive while riding out this hurricane like a sea turtle hanging on for dear life to a battered and blistered palm tree.

At that moment in time, hanging up the phone was the nicest thing I could do for everyone.

Thank God, our cat lived and bounced back after his vet came through the next day. The nurse even delivered it to us at home and said to just pay when we could.

You see, compassion is relevant. Circumstances are relevant.

The amount of information you have about someone's life is relevant. It's really not hard to find compassion for someone when you know the whole story. And yet, we are each accountable and responsible in choosing our "what now."

I believe Ms. Comuckle deserved the benefit of context. Even if Jack wasn't his usual imposing and intimidating, official-government-business personality, perhaps there was something more going on with Ms. Comuckle than tall grass and an overflowing trash barrel in her front yard. Had she just lost her husband? A child? Was she ill? Where were the answers to those questions in Jack's investigation? And compassion? Clearly, if it existed, it wasn't documented, and certainly not exercised. And yet, as a citizen of the community, she was still responsible for maintaining her lawn and keeping her property garbage-free.

As for the emergency veterinary clinic's secretary, I think it's fair for me to suspend my judgment on that entire scenario because people just can't know what they don't know, and even if the secretary did know, there may not have been much in her power to do anything differently or offer me any other answers. The Truth is, I'm 100% responsible for my reaction to anyone or anything. I'm 100% responsible for my own part in all things. We're all accountable for what we say, what we do, and how we respond, but don't you think there are situations that deserve the benefit of compassionate context? I do.

I think you deserve that kind of compassion, too. Yes, you.

Have you ever . . . (*choose all that apply, feel free to add on*):

a) Cut someone off in traffic accidentally?
b) Run a red light?
c) Yelled at your kids?
d) Cussed someone in traffic?
e) Been snippy with someone who didn't deserve it?
f) Lied about why you were late?
g) Rolled through a stop sign?
h) Lied about why you weren't going to be there?
i) Arrived late to an appointment or meeting?
j) Married the wrong person?
k) Become super-duper pissed off in a retail store?
l) Lost it on a customer service person over the phone?
m) Yelled at your spouse?
n) Blamed the dog for the smell?
o) Pretended you didn't see the text message?
p) Ate your kid's candy?
q) Hid the wrapper?
r)
s)
t)
u)
v)
w)
x)
y)
z)

Why in the world would you ever do any of those things? I mean, come on. Really? *You?*

If you answered yes to any of those things (or filled in the blanks with some of your own), and these things are clearly not on your list of best moments—and you would, in fact, go back and edit those out of your history if you could, welcome to the party. We've all done something well beneath our own personal standards, and we're usually very willing to kick our own asses for a long time after the circumstance has passed, and often without giving ourselves the benefit of context. This isn't to say we're not accountable for our actions. You don't get to make excuses to wave away your own, personal accountability. If you can make amends, do that. If you must simply do better by plugging yourself in to what's driving your frustrations or avoidances, yes, please do look into it, but above all, be honest with yourself. When you've asked for forgiveness from the people you love, it's time to offer yourself some grace, too.

In criminal and civil trials, they use what is called the reasonable person standard. They use a hypothetical person they call a "reasonable person," who, "exercises average care, skill, and judgment in conduct," and then compare them to the person on trial to determine liability. They ask, would a reasonable person in the same or similar circumstances respond in a similar way?

So, before you put yourself on trial for the rest of your life for something that was so out of character for you, something that's hard for even you to believe that you did it, it's worth considering if, perhaps, you were having a normal reaction to very abnormal circumstances.

That is the beginning of self-compassion, and the reservoir from which your compassion for others can flow.

With it, you can bend. Without it, you may break.

BECOMING YOUR OWN TRUTHFAIRY

MISSION SIX: For the next 24 hours, take notice of the people you engage, witness, or encounter.

At the end of the day, pick the one person who stood out to you in a most aggravating, annoying, or frustrating way, and give them a really descriptive cartoon mobster name like, *Barbie the Banshee*, or *Jimmy the Jerk*.

STRONG SUGGESTION FOR BEST RESULTS:
Leave your family and/or former family members out of this one.

When you've had your fun with that, ask yourself the following questions about this character you've created.

1. Is this the actual name that appears on this person's birth certificate?

2. Are you *experiencing* Barbie as a banshee and Jimmy as a jerk, or do you *know* they are *actually* and *completely* a banshee and a jerk every day of their life (and you know it for sure)?

3. Now, think of three possible scenarios that Jimmy and Barbie may have, or are currently enduring that could make a reasonable person behave in ways that match the name you gave them.

Once I know who I'm not, then I'll know who I am.
-Alanis Morissette

AND ONE MORE THING

I feel like I need to say something before we finish up this first Truthfairy volume.

I'm not *the* Truthfairy.

It's above my pay grade, and the pageant sash for that title is too heavy for anyone to wear. This book is about becoming a Truthfairy—for yourself, and others. Deciding to be a Truthfairy was a natural awakening that was always there waiting for me to recognize, learn about, and experience. Becoming a Truthfairy is about looking in the mirror and being compassionately honest with yourself and being trustworthy to yourself, first. That's where it all begins. Are you reliable to tell yourself the truth about how you feel, what you think, what you believe, and maybe even why? Understand, this isn't a question of whether you're willing to write a tell-all exposé on yourself to sell on Amazon, post about it on Facebook, or even share what you think or feel with anyone else right away. I'm asking you if you're willing to speak the truth about things to yourself—if even, for now, just the little ones?

And, about being a Truthfairy for others.

I want to point out again that this means being a compassionate witness who is willing to acknowledge someone else's truth when they speak it. You don't have to agree (because you won't always), you most certainly should not transition into therapist mode (because that's not what this is about)— just be a compassionate witness that is willing to see, hear, and know the human soul you're in front of, if only for that moment.

To be truly witnessed is to be seen, known, heard. That's all any of us really wants, even when, at the same time, it seems like the scariest thing that could happen. When two trustworthy souls can meet one another in dignity, respect, and acknowledgement, it changes the way we see one another. When your trustworthy soul meets another trustworthy soul with dignity, respect, and acknowledgement, it changes everything.

Tell your Truth. You deserve to hear it from you.

BECOMING YOUR VERY OWN TRUTHFAIRY

MISSION SEVEN (*have fun with this one*): Pick a stage name, a pen name, a super-hero style alter-ego name, an honorary Powerpuff Girl moniker, any beautiful name you choose to identify all your shiniest, beautiful qualities with. This is the name you'd want everyone on the recess playground to call you, if even for just one day.

Don't make this too hard.

If by the end of recess, the name you picked doesn't suit you, pick a different one for tomorrow.

⌇

Your Truthfairy Experience has begun, and here we are.

No guru required.

BONUS MISSION: Now that you're here, tell yourself one more Truth. Just one more, little, compassionate Truth you have never said out loud before.

Just tell it to yourself.

Rinse and repeat for the next seven days. (Yes, in a row.)

P.S. Now that we've come full-circle, I'd love to hear about how you are experiencing this journey after these first seven little missions.

What was it like *for you*? How far have you come?
Where did you dive in the deepest?
What do you feel?
What did you resist?
Email me at Truthfairy@TheNorthArrow.com
(Yes, really.)

You don't have to be fearless. Just sincere.
-Danielle LaPorte

DEAR TRUTHFAIRY . . .

For each time you dusted the dirt from the seat of your pants;

Each pleading prayer and every hand raised toward heaven
in staggering gratitude;

For every time you wiped the sweat from your brow;

Every time compassion met you at the depth of your pain;

For every time you broke through a finish line chest-first–or
with bleeding elbows on your hands and knees;

For each time you re-gathered your lost marbles and started
playing with your full deck again;

For every compassionate hand you have held and offered;

For every illusion revealed;

For every time you spoke your Truth on your own behalf, and it freed you;

For every sacred moment you recognize in real time;

For each moment of terror;

For every time you went on a recon mission to save yourself;

For each time you chose to keep trying to breathe even when the air would not flow in;

For every tear-soaked pillow smeared with gooey snot;

Every butt-clenching close call;

Every time your gut laughter could not heed your bladder's final warning;

For each time Love surprised you like a sweepstakes prize;

The time they played your song—full blast;

For every time your whimsy took over;

For each time the Truth seemed to hurt;

For every *can't* you argued against;

Each time the sunrise paused your world;

For each and every time your Truth served you,
and for each moment you agreed to honor it.

Keep your North, my friend, and keep going ...
you're writing a most epic story all the world needs.

That's something I've been waiting to tell you.

What I know for sure is ...
your freedom is in your Truth.

To be continued,
Donna

NOW, THEN . . .

Since we're here together, I'd really like to tell you about this thing. I mentioned it at the front of the book, but in case you missed it, you're invited to join us over here:

www.TRUTHFAIRYEXPERIENCE.com

The Truthfairy Experience™ is part of the next steps in your practice of becoming your own Truthfairy.

I created it with my heart, especially for us so we can start connecting with even more women just like us, who have been where you are and will help you remember what you already know, and might have just forgotten. Join a community of compassionate witnesses who are here to be part of your growth and your rising, even if you're showing up with skinned knees.

Along my own Yellow Brick Road adventure, I realized that I'm not alone in the search for other aware and compassionate women. Women who are interested in getting to the

Truth about themselves and their relationships with others—especially those who are no longer satisfied with *pretending not to know* what they know.

The Truth is . . . there is more for you.
More for all of us.

I think it's time women learn how to better speak and own their Truth without fear. If you're up for the journey to dive deeper and fly higher, you're my kind of gal.

First of all, are we *Your* kind?

- Are you open to seeing yourself?
- Do you suspect there's more for you to be/do/live in this lifetime?
- Tired of pretending you're absolutely glued-together (like all the other women you "know" about)?
- Ever wondered if you're riding the crazy train and no one else is noticing but you?
- Are you hell-bent on getting down to business about who in the world you are?
- You're ready to face yourself, get to know yourself *even more* while you continue claiming the life you are meant to live.

If any of the above is a *yes* for you . . .

YOU ARE PERSONALLY INVITED

www.TruthfairyExperience.com

My Dear School Teachers,

Just before this book was transferred into the pre-print ironing board, I was sitting at my kitchen table creating swirly-glittery-glowing Dream Jars for my younger children's most loving teachers. On a Tuesday morning, just before winter break, I had three fingers and one thumb covered with Serious Glue™ (the pet name I have for crazy glue that works with glass), surrounded by eleven containers of ultra-fine glitter—gold, silver, purple, aqua, alongside blues and purples of three different hues. So far, none had spilled beyond the piece of paper I was using to catch the overflow.

As I was swirling glitter, I thought about each teacher my kids love, and why. I realized the teachers they love are those my children feel most loved *by*—so much so, that they asked me to make Dream Jars gifts for them. Now, unless you've watched Disney's *BFG-Big Friendly Giant*, you might not know what a Dream Jar is, but if have, you'll know it's a precious notion that represents the wishes that your heart makes. When I'm making a Dream Jar, I'm thinking of no one but the person it is for.

Today, as I was making them for their teachers, memories of my own grade school teachers started to mingle in—tears rolled like credits into streams of melted mascara down my face. The scene would not have been complete had I not spilled a pile of glitter down the front of my pajamas. Totally worth it.

Because good teachers are special people.

~

Today, I call the names of my own teachers.

Ms. Jaqueline LaMountain, who would smile at me in church, and for that Kindergarten song about colors I still know all the words to.

Ms. Mary Jo Manuel who taught me how to tell time.

Ms. Mary Harper, who recognized my gift for remembering things, who is responsible for my beautiful handwriting, and who honored me with my first Certificate of Achievement award for, "Self-Improvement." Rest in Peace, sweet Mrs. Harper.

Mr. Daniel Stanley who knew more about me than he let on and who was a powerfully quiet man who knew how to disarm bullies like a Vulcan. Rest in Precious Peace, Mr. Stanley.

Ms. Sue Gorker, who taught me about brain science, healing, and feelings, as she unlocked my fascination with all things mathematical. Her brightness is from beyond this world.

Mr. Doug Day, who told the Truth, was my first maître d' of psychology, and who opened our minds to seeing the bigger world. Have I now got some books for *him* to read over tea and crumpets.

Dear Teachers, I have experienced each of you as navigation stars along my journey back to my whole self. You were examples of sanity in a world I didn't understand.

And to all our Teachers, you are our hope, because sometimes, a teacher is the only adult a child has to hold on to—and you may never know which child it turns out to be.

The children who need you will never forget.

UP NEXT: TRUTHFAIRY FIELD GUIDE VOLUME 2

You've done so much good for yourself, and the better news is, there's more for you.

Ready to dive in a little deeper? Get ready to create your personal BOUNDARY MAP™, start slaying your inner LYING HYDRA, learn three-steps to finally TRUSTING YOURSELF, how to stop PRETENDING NOT TO KNOW, and how to shift from COMPETING to CONNECTING with yourself and others.

We can do this together, Truthfairy.

In fact, we're doing it right now.

BOOKS THAT HELPED ME GET HERE FASTER

Bird by Bird
Anne Lamott
Fairy Godmother of Writers To-Be

The Firestarter Sessions
Danielle LaPorte
Igniter of Truth Bombs

Big Magic
Elizabeth Gilbert
Ooooey-Gooey Inspiration Sparker

You Are a Badass
Jen Sincero
Heavy Weight (it's all muscle) *Champion of Doubt-Busting*

Warrior of the Light, as told by Paulo Coelho, after he taught me *The Alchemist*

The Fonzi of Researchers, Dr. Brené Brown of *Daring Greatly*

Diana Herself
Transcribed and Midwifed by Herself, Martha Beck

Drum Major of Trauma Recovery, Dr. Bessel van der Kolk, *The Body Keeps the Score*

PEOPLE WHOSE WORK I HAVE FAN-GIRLED

Dancing Queen **Marie Forleo**, and her straight-up *B-School,* because, "Everything is figure-outable."

The Lodestar of Business Sermons, **Gary Vaynerchuk** of *Vayner Media,* Elvis would have loved you.

Sylvester Stallone, for never letting go of *Rocky.*

Queen Ellen of Kindness, for *Finding Dory.*

And of course, **Oprah**, the *Grand Empress of I Can.*

LONG-DISTANCE DEDICATION MUSIC
TO MYSELF, FROM MYSELF

Alanis Morissette, *Supposed Former Infatuation Junkie*, and that *Jagged Little Pill*, through the *Prayer Cycle,* all the way to *Havoc and Bright Lights . . . Thank U*, your gospel music and I, we have traveled far.

The poet laureate of love songs, the guy who wrote in such a way that I was willing to believe the kind of romantic love he sings about might actually be real, especially at a time when I had experienced no evidence of it and very little reason to believe, thank you in all the ways for your *Fields of Gold* and *Brand New Day*: **Gordon Mathew Thomas Sumner, The Sting.**

To **Ms. Beyoncé** for letting us know, without a doubt, what time it is—check.

And to the *Divine Ms. M*, the *Fairy Godmother of Truthfairy Anthems*, **The Bette Midler.** Thank you for every theme song and lullaby I ever sang with you in the mirror.

A PLACE TO WRITE

NOTES

NOTES

AND, MORE NOTES . . .

ABOUT THE AUTHOR

DONNA SYED designs and facilitates experiential trainings for women, helping them discover their own brilliant, *capital-T* Truths. Donna is an inspirational speaker, somatic dance practitioner, founder of the *Truthfairy Experience*™ and *Awaken Women Dance*™. She has been a featured "Truthteller" at *Women For One*, a contributor to *Psych-Central,* and *The Huffington Post* while also a wife and mother of four. From the middle of America, she's a little bit Lucy Ricardo with a dash of Gump, and prefers ruby house slippers over any other shoe.

For more information
www.DonnaSyed.com
Truthfairy@TheNorthArrow.com

Made in the USA
San Bernardino, CA
02 February 2018